# Fifth Grade Workbooks

# Sequencing & Memory Practice

BABY PROFESSOR
EDUCATION KIDS

Speedy Publishing LLC
40 E. Main St. #1156
Newark, DE 19711
www.speedypublishing.com

The human brain is like a powerful computer that stores our memory and controls how we as humans think and react.

On the next few pages are challenges and games to test your memory! Enjoy!

# Instructions:

Repeat the sequence of numbers shown by writing the numbers at the back of the page. Challenge yourself! Do not simply copy!

Level 1
119346

# LEVEL 1

## Answer:

_______________

# Level 2

2394679

# LEVEL 2

## Answer:

________________________________

Level 3
77933296

# LEVEL 3

## Answer:

_______________

# Level 4

334006991

# LEVEL 4
## Answer:

______________________

Level 5
0002234934

# LEVEL 5

## Answer:

_______________

Level 6
001931731 9

# LEVEL 6

## Answer:

_______________

Level 7
8897334642

# LEVEL 7

## Answer:

_______________________

# Level 8

079385462 9

# LEVEL 8
## Answer:

_______________

Level 9
2143647932

# LEVEL 9
## Answer:

_______________

# Level 10

4976594231

# LEVEL 10

## Answer:

_______________

A sequence is an ordered collection of objects in which repetitions are allowed. Like a set, it contains members (also called elements, or terms). The number of elements (possibly infinite) is called the length of the sequence.

# Instructions:

Memorize the sequence of objects and on the next page, encircle which of the set is not on the correct placement.

# Test 1

# Test 2

# Didn't get everything correct?

It's typical for people to forget more things as they grow older. Your parents or grandparents might joke about having a "senior moment." That's when they forget something.